19,96

KATE DICAMILLO
NEWBERY MEDAL–WINNING AUTHOR

THERESE SHEA

Britannica®
Educational Publishing

IN ASSOCIATION WITH

ROSEN
EDUCATIONAL SERVICES

Published in 2016 by Britannica Educational Publishing (a trademark of Encyclopædia Britannica, Inc.) in association with The Rosen Publishing Group, Inc.
29 East 21st Street, New York, NY 10010

Distributed exclusively by Rosen Publishing.
To see additional Britannica Educational Publishing titles, go to rosenpublishing.com.

First Edition

Britannica Educational Publishing
J. E. Luebering: Director, Core Reference Group
Mary Rose McCudden: Editor, Britannica Student Encyclopedia

Rosen Publishing
Hope Lourie Killcoyne: Executive Editor
Christine Poolos: Editor
Nelson Sá: Art Director
Michael Moy: Designer
Cindy Reiman: Photography Manager

Library of Congress Cataloging-in-Publication Data

Shea, Therese.
Kate DiCamillo: Newbery Medal–winning author/Therese Shea.—First edition.
      pages cm.—(Britannica beginner bios)
Includes bibliographical references and index.
ISBN 978-1-62275-936-1 (library bound)—ISBN 978-1-62275-937-8 (pbk.)—ISBN 978-1-62275-939-2 (6-pack)
1. DiCamillo, Kate—Juvenile literature. 2. Authors, American—21st century—Biography—Juvenile literature. 3. Children's stories—Authorship—Juvenile literature. I. Title.
PS3604.I23Z86 2016
813'.6—dc23
[B]

2014039763

Manufactured in the United States of America

CONTENTS

"STORIES ARE EVERYWHERE"

Kate DiCamillo is the author of many popular children's and young adult books. Her novels often center on important real-life **THEMES**, such as death, separation, and loss. These themes are not often in books for younger people. However, DiCamillo understands that many young people go through hard times. She did. She wants

Kate DiCamillo's love of reading and writing shines through in her books.

her readers to see themselves in her characters. DiCamillo also writes funny books for younger readers.

Kate DiCamillo did not have an easy path to success. Though she was always a talented writer, she had to make herself write every day. It took her years to learn to do this. She also had to deal with rejections from publishing companies. However, she kept trying until her work was accepted.

DiCamillo says that a book is not complete until someone reads it!

DiCamillo sees stories in her surroundings and in the people who pass her by on the street.

DiCamillo's struggles with writing can teach those who want to be authors about the process. She has also offered advice to future writers. She says, "Stories are everywhere. All you have to do is pay attention."

Quick Fact

On her website, Kate DiCamillo tells her fans about herself: "I am short. And loud. I hate to cook and love to eat." She calls herself a "storyteller."

CHAPTER TWO

BECOMING A WRITER

Katrina Elizabeth "Kate" DiCamillo was born on March 25, 1964, in Philadelphia, Pennsylvania. Kate had **CHRONIC PNEUMONIA** when she was young. She was often sick. Her doctors suggested that the family move to a warmer place. When Kate was five years old, she moved with her mother and older

Vocabulary

CHRONIC PNEUMONIA is an illness of the lungs that lasts for a long time or keeps coming back. People with chronic pneumonia may cough, run a fever, and have a hard time breathing.

The move to Florida changed Kate DiCamillo's life.

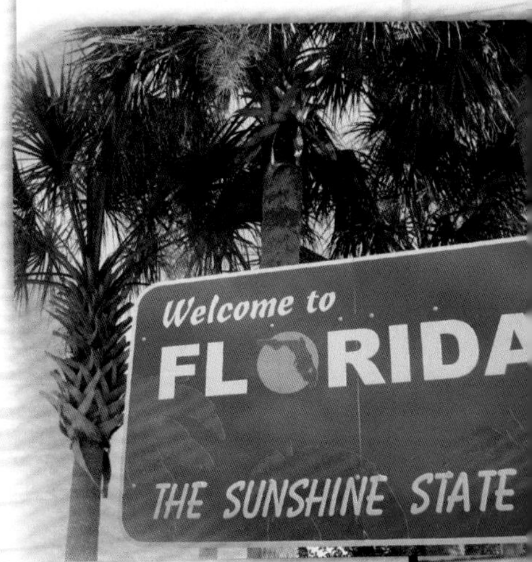

Welcome to
FLORIDA
THE SUNSHINE STATE

brother to Clermont, Florida. Her father stayed in Pennsylvania. He said he would join them later but never did. Kate and her family believed for a long time that he was coming. She would later write about children with missing parents and how they dealt with their feelings.

This is an illustration of a scene from one of Kate's favorite books, *The Secret Garden*.

Kate spent a lot of time sick in bed in Florida. However, she used her imagination and read a lot. Some of her favorite books as a young girl were *The Twenty-One Balloons*, *The Secret Garden*, *The Yearling*, *Ribsy*, and *Somebody Else's Shoes*. She began to want to be a writer.

Years later, DiCamillo went to college at the University of Florida at Gainesville. She took writing classes there. Her teachers told her she had talent. After school, DiCamillo thought she was going to be a writer. She believed it would just happen naturally. To earn money, she had many jobs. She even worked at Disney World for

One of the many jobs DiCamillo had before becoming a writer was helping people on rides at Disney World.

DiCamillo hopes that all children can develop a love of reading, as she did.

Expedited

DiCamillo worked at a book warehouse like this one for several years.

a time. DiCamillo did not actually start to write until she was about 29. At first, she wrote several short stories for adults.

In 1994, DiCamillo thought she needed a change. She moved to Minnesota with a friend. There, she took a job at a book warehouse. She worked more than four

Quick Fact

Kate DiCamillo studied *The Watsons Go to Birmingham—1963*, a young adult book by Christopher Paul Curtis. She even typed out pages of the book to better understand how he wrote.

years in the children's books section. She fell in love with the children's **FICTION** she read there. She began to think about trying to write a children's story of her own.

DiCamillo began to write in the mornings, before she went to work. She sent her work to publishing companies. She received many rejection letters—as many as four hundred! However, Kate DiCamillo did not give up.

Vocabulary

FICTION is a made-up story about imaginary people and events.

BREAKTHROUGH BOOK

The cold Minnesota winter made DiCamillo miss the Florida sunshine.

During a cold winter in Minnesota, DiCamillo was homesick for Florida. She was lonely and missed having a dog around. Since she could not travel home and could not have a dog, she wrote a children's **NOVEL** set in Florida about her idea of the perfect dog.

Vocabulary

A **NOVEL** is a long story that usually portrays imaginary characters and events.

In the Milwaukee newspaper *The Journal Sentinel*, DiCamillo told more about where her ideas came from: "One night before I went to sleep I heard a little girl's voice with a Southern accent say, 'I have a dawg named Winn-Dixie.' . . . I started with that sentence and that voice."

DiCamillo's story is about a young girl named Opal who moves to Florida with her father. The lonely girl finds a dog in the grocery store. She brings him home and names him Winn-Dixie, after the store where she found him. During one special summer, Opal learns about her missing mother, how to make new friends, and how to forgive others.

DiCamillo poses with the dog that played Winn-Dixie in the movie based on her book.

DiCamillo called her story *Because of Winn-Dixie.* When she finished writing it, she sent the **MANUSCRIPT** to an editor at Candlewick Press. Unfortunately, the editor was out of the office for several months. The manuscript became buried under a pile of other manuscripts. Then, a young editor found it. She loved the story and showed it to her boss. The editor began to work with DiCamillo to get the book ready for publishing. It was her first book as an editor and DiCamillo's first book as an author.

> **Vocabulary**
>
> **A MANUSCRIPT is a written or typewritten story. An author sends a manuscript to a publishing company to be made into a book.**

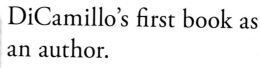

Editors' desks are often covered in manuscripts.

In 2000, *Because of Winn-Dixie* was published. The book quickly became very popular. One morning in early 2001, DiCamillo got a telephone call telling her that *Because of Winn-Dixie* had won an award called a Newbery Honor. She said in the *Orlando Sentinel* newspaper, "I used to go the library and look for those books with the Newbery seal on them. And I couldn't believe my first book would win such an honor."

It is unusual for a writer to win an award for her first book—but DiCamillo did.

15

Through her success, DiCamillo had discovered that writing is more about hard work than talent. So, she kept writing and set goals for herself. She wrote at least two pages every morning, before other things came up in her day. DiCamillo said that she never felt like writing but was always glad she did. She loved it when a story was finally done. And she had many more stories to finish.

Quick Fact

The Newbery Awards are the best-known children's book awards in the United States. The Newbery Medal is the highest award. Newbery Honors are given to a few other worthy books each year.

CHAPTER FOUR

MORE BESTSELLERS

DiCamillo signs a book for a fan.

About a year after *Because of Winn-Dixie* was published, Kate DiCamillo completed her second book, *The Tiger Rising*. The story focuses on Rob, a boy whose mother has died of cancer. Rob keeps his feelings inside. One day, he finds a tiger in a cage in the woods. This event and his friendship with a classmate named Sistine help Rob deal with his pain.

DiCamillo chose a hard real-life theme—how a young person deals with losing a parent. She saw herself in Sistine, the girl who asks Rob to be more open. Sistine believes that she will soon live with her father, which is not possible. Both characters end up helping each other. *The Tiger Rising* won many fans. It was a National Book Award finalist.

DiCamillo has said she listens to her characters when writing her books. She is sometimes surprised where they take her in a story. She often gets

Not all of DiCamillo's characters are people. Despereaux is a mouse!

Vocabulary
To **ILLUSTRATE** is to draw pictures for a book that explain or decorate the story.

ideas for them from the real world, though. A college teacher told DiCamillo that good writing is about paying close attention to the people and places around us. That is how DiCamillo creates such lifelike characters and stories.

DiCamillo's next book came from another person's imagination. A friend's son asked her to write about an unlikely hero with large ears. With that picture in her mind, she wrote *The Tale of Despereaux: Being the Story of a Mouse, a Princess, Some Soup, and a Spool of Thread*. It was **ILLUSTRATED** by Timothy Basil Ering and published in 2003. The hero is Despereaux Tilling, a mouse born in a castle who loves music and stories. Despereaux's bravery is tested as he tries to save a princess. He meets a rat named Roscuro and a servant girl, Miggery, along the way.

Quick Fact

Two of DiCamillo's books have been made into movies. *Because of Winn-Dixie* came out in 2005, and *The Tale of Despereaux*, an animated movie, came out in 2008.

Despereaux's story won the Newbery Medal for best children's book for 2004. On her website, DiCamillo wrote: "It was the most amazing, unbelievable, wonderful, fantastic, extra-ordinary thing. Truthfully, I still can't believe it."

Many of DiCamillo's other stories and characters come from images in her mind or in the world around her. One day, a friend was describing how much she loved toast. Later, DiCamillo wrote several chapter books for beginning

DiCamillo stands with a costume character version of Despereaux.

Quick Fact

Kate DiCamillo writes the Bink & Gollie chapter book series with Alison McGhee. These books are illustrated by Tony Fucile. The series centers on two smart girls and their funny adventures.

readers about a pig, Mercy Watson, who loves toast. The first was *Mercy Watson to the Rescue* (2005), which was illustrated by Chris Van Dusen.

DiCamillo's novel *The Miraculous Journey of Edward Tulane* (2006) is about a hard-hearted china rabbit who learns how to love. DiCamillo thought of the story when she had a dream about a rabbit doll that someone had given her. She truly keeps an open mind when she is looking for new ideas.

DiCamillo talks with a group of fans at a bookstore.

CHAPTER FIVE

READING AMBASSADOR

Even though Kate DiCamillo is a successful author, she has continued to live a normal life. She still gets up early in the morning to make herself write. DiCamillo has said that her writing is usually not perfect the first time, so she is always rewriting. She

DiCamillo is shown here with Henry, her family's dog.

KATE DiCAMILLO

The MIRACULOUS JOURNEY of EDWARD TULANE

Edward Tulane is a china rabbit who learns how to love.

once said that she rewrites her books eight or more times!

When DiCamillo wants to relax, she spends time with friends and family. She loves to be with her nephews and niece. They share a dog named Henry, who is a bit like Winn-Dixie.

In addition to novels and chapter books, DiCamillo writes picture books. She writes the words and other people make the drawings. *Great Joy*, illustrated by Bagram Ibatoulline, was published in 2007. *Louise: The Adventures of a Chicken*, illustrated by Harry Bliss, was published in 2008. DiCamillo said she finds these books harder to write than novels and chapter books. There are few words, so every word is important and must be perfectly placed.

Kate DiCamillo again tried something new with *Flora & Ulysses: The Illuminated Adventures*. The book tells the story of a young comic-book lover and a squirrel with human abilities. It has comic-style pictures as well as full-page illustrations, the work of artist K. G. Campbell. The novel was published in 2013. It was awarded the Newbery Medal in 2014.

Vocabulary

An **AMBASSADOR** is someone who acts as an official representative or messenger for a cause or a group of people.

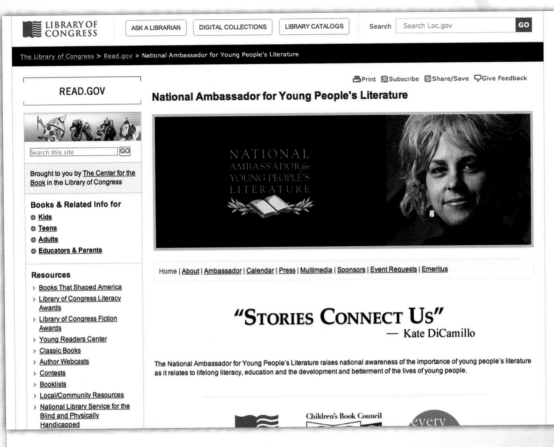

DiCamillo traveled and talked to many young people through her job as an ambassador for literature.

That same year, Kate DiCamillo received another great honor. She was named the national **AMBASSADOR** for young people's literature by the

DiCamillo continues to grow as a writer, always trying new things.

Library of Congress. Her job was to travel around the country for two years to tell others how important reading is. Reading books helped her through her childhood illnesses and gave her hope for a future as a writer.

In her role as an ambassador, DiCamillo shared her life story as well as her books with young people. She encouraged them to read and write, as she did and still does. They, too, may become authors of award-winning books!

Kate DiCamillo's books are popular around the world. They have been translated into more than

> **Quick Fact**
> As ambassador, DiCamillo promotes the idea that stories can connect us: "When we read together . . . we are taken out of our aloneness. Together, we see the world. Together, we see one another. We connect. And when we connect, we are changed."

Kate DiCamillo's stories have entertained people around the world.

30 languages and have sold millions of copies. She has said, "I think of myself as an enormously lucky person: I get to tell stories for a living." Her many fans feel lucky she tells those stories.

TIMELINE

1964: Kate DiCamillo is born on March 25 in Philadelphia, Pennsylvania.

1969: DiCamillo moves to Florida.

1987: DiCamillo graduates from the University of Florida at Gainesville, where she took writing courses.

1994: DiCamillo moves to Minnesota.

2000: DiCamillo's first book, *Because of Winn-Dixie*, is published.

2001: *Because of Winn-Dixie* wins a Newbery Honor.

2001: *The Tiger Rising* is published.

2003: *The Tale of Despereaux* is published.

2004: *The Tale of Despereaux* is awarded the Newbery Medal.

2005: *Because of Winn-Dixie* is released as a movie.

2005: The first Mercy Watson chapter book, *Mercy Watson to the Rescue*, comes out.

2006: The novel *The Miraculous Journey of Edward Tulane* is published.

2006: *The Miraculous Journey of Edward Tulane* receives the Boston Globe–Horn Book Award for Fiction.

2007: DiCamillo's first picture book, *Great Joy*, is published.

2008: DiCamillo's picture book *Louise: The Adventures of a Chicken* is published.

2008: *The Tale of Despereaux* movie is released.

2009: The novel *The Magician's Elephant* is published.

2010: *Bink & Gollie* is published. It is the first of a series authored by DiCamillo and Alison McGhee. It will go on to win the Theodor Seuss Geisel Medal.

2013: *Flora & Ulysses: The Illuminated Adventures* is published. It will be DiCamillo's second book to be awarded the Newbery Medal.

2014: Kate DiCamillo is named the national ambassador for young people's literature by the Library of Congress.

GLOSSARY

ACCENT A way of talking shared by a group, such as the people of a country.

ADVICE Someone's opinion about what another person should do.

ANIMATED Made up of a series of pictures or drawings that seem to move when shown one after another very quickly.

EDITOR Someone who is in charge of getting a book ready for public use.

LITERATURE Important written works.

PUBLISHING The business of preparing and making books and other written works that will be supplied to the public.

REJECTION The act of refusing to accept something.

SEPARATION The state of being apart from someone or something.

TRANSLATE To give the meaning of something in another language.

WAREHOUSE A large building in which goods are stored.

FOR MORE INFORMATION

BOOKS

Corbett, Sue. *Kate DiCamillo*. New York, NY: Marshall Cavendish Benchmark, 2013.

Minden, Cecilia, and Kate Roth. *How to Write About Your Adventure*. Ann Arbor, MI: Cherry Lake Publishing, 2012.

Wheeler, Jill C. *Kate DiCamillo*. Edina, MN: ABDO Publishing, 2009.

WEBSITES

Because of the changing nature of Internet links, Rosen Publishing has developed an online list of websites related to the subject of this book. This site is updated regularly. Please use this link to access this list:

http://www.rosenlinks.com/BBB/DiCam

INDEX